T0148496

A Flame of Fire
Joseph Goodman

"Who maketh his angels spirits; his
ministers a flaming fire"-Psalm 104:4

authorHOUSE®

AuthorHouse™
1663 Liberty Drive
Bloomington, IN 47403
www.authorhouse.com
Phone: 1-800-839-8640

Published by AuthorHouse 2/4/2013

ISBN: 978-1-4817-1319-1 (sc)
ISBN: 978-1-4817-1320-7 (e)

A Note from the Author

My name is Joseph Sean Goodman and I was once one of the billions of stars that you look up and see at night, one day my flame seemed to burn out and I found myself falling as fast as I could to the ground. I've been divorced, poisoned and left for dead, held at gun point, and forced to do drugs. I married again and my wife passed away, my kids that I had raised for nine long years were taken away, I sold drugs to survive, I had a habit of drinking and smoking marijuana daily, taking prescription pills and snorting powder four times a week, and smoking crack. But God saved me and has delivered me there's still a lot of work to be done but I am striving to make heaven my home one day. I don't have much of an education and most of the words I have written are incorrect and had to be rewritten. I was diagnosed with paranoid schizophrenia I have anxiety attacks and maybe you want to judge me, maybe you would say what does he know? And you're right I don't have the education or the degree but I promise you this book will help you understand you and maybe you will ask the question where did I go wrong and how do I get my flame back?

As I wrote this book it was very important for me to add God into some of these pages. I needed to explain that having a God in your life or something to hold you accountable is one of the greatest secrets of staying centered. No matter what God you serve it's important to think of a higher power. One who judges our actions because we couldn't discipline ourselves. To think we are our Gods is not the way it is intended to be if you want to change your actions. I was raised to believe in Jesus. To change from this belief would be very hard as well as some of you changing your beliefs. But who is God? There are many disagreements. What we can agree on is we are very emotional people; to even speak against someone's God means we are ready to fight.

As a paranoid Schizophrenic I feel every emotion, sometimes all at once and I had to practice showing different feelings at the appropriate times because I could not recognize which emotion I was feeling. I know in me and in others the source of our problems come from a lack of social skills as children. If you think about it we are all weak in some areas because we didn't fully develop as children or interact with others to develop certain skills. For example, I never crossed a milestone in my life, not even kindergarten; I never stood in front of a crowd of people, or gave a speech to a group. As a result I lack social skills and have extreme stage fright. For me to do a speech would mean I am in unchartered waters.

The reason I speak so much of religion and church is because even if you are atheist you believe in a higher power, even if its aliens. We must hold fast to this belief because with anything we develop a sense of doing right, a sense of what is wrong, and most of all there are consequences. Without this belief we would be no different than the cavemen before us and unless America embraces all religion and beliefs with the history and research to back it up, not just something made up; we will continue to let our emotions rule our actions. I was one of those guys who just did what felt right at that time. Imagine, I am schizophrenic so what may feel right to me may look stupid to everyone else. I was at the point of going completely manic or just losing myself to what I felt, heard, or saw which made me become uncontrollable. When this would happen to me I would imagine what I was taught of as a child. I would envision a God who was all powerful, had wisdom, and peace, and endless love. I created an image of someone perfect; I started to follow his standards and I'm a better person for it. I still have all the emotional problems but I've learned how to cope with them, I have learned from them by reflecting what a feeling means and I hold myself accountable for my own actions; and you know what? I wouldn't change a thing now.

Trapped by Sin or Wrongful Actions (A parable)

There have been many stories about wild animals getting caught into different kinds of traps. What comes to mind mostly for me is the bear trap, there may be no food to lure the animal but the trapper doesn't even care what animal he may capture all he can see is profit. If he can claim the skin he can make money at the animals' expense. The trap has no respected thing, it would even trap humans. What comes to mind when we think about an animal in a trap is how an animal will make a choice to both stay in the trap and perish, or to chew off its own member and live. The moral of this story is what do you value most? What will you give up? And is the pain worth your life? Because the wages of sin or wrongful actions is death (Romans 6:23).

In Luke 15:11 the prodigal son started out on a journey with a pocket full of money; he stood tall and his head held high. As he walked in to the town he probably seen things he had never seen before: gambling, dancing, drunkenness, and lewd women. With all of the money, it was easy to find friends. I would not dare to say he went looking for sin, but simply looking for something besides what he had. Trying to make his own path, make his own fortune, and find his own way. But somewhere in finding his new way he became trapped and couldn't find a way out of the situation he had got himself in.

Like the animal, when you become trapped for a few days laying in your mess, when all your money is gone and your friends and on top of it all you get hungry. Your stomach starts to growl like an angry bear and you start to talk to yourself because now you think you're going to die. When this happens you may start weighing out your options. What can you live without? When you decide what you can live without it is a good feeling, but you know it's going to hurt.

The prodigal son found himself in the pigpen, eating the same slop the swine ate. He knew his only option was to face his shame and go back home. He went back to his father just as humble and contrite as you could have ever imagined the story of his past showing in his eyes. His father met him, embraced him, and restored him as his son he did not turn his back or say I told you so he loved him and accepted him just as he did before. Just like our God does for us all we have to do is forgive and accept that we are not always right and sometimes father really does know best.

Who said you have to have it?

"If I don't have it I will die!" food, drink, cravings, lust, drugs; all these are things that at one time we may have thought we had to have to survive. If our body yearns for something it produces a feeling of worrisome nagging discomfort, a physical hurt. When this feeling hits we know we want whatever it is more than anything else in the world at that moment. People have traded their bodies, money, kids, and cars; they have stolen, borrowed, or rented things just to fix that desire for that day.

It's natural to feel these ways toward an object or

thing besides your human. If you stayed outside in the mud and dirt and never bathed or cleaned yourself you would be filthy. But if you washed yourself, soaked, and scrubbed and wiped away all of your filth you would be clean. It takes effort and sometimes it can hurt. Have you ever washed grease off your hands? When you go to scrub at the grime you can sometimes scrub the skin right off! Have you ever been so tired you didn't even feel like bathing? It takes an effort physically, mentally, and spiritually. But where's your fight? Where is your desire to change? Where is your hunger to see God move in your life? Where is your thirst to see the miracles to know you believed and trusted God for something and he come through for you?

We need to be more like Jacob, in Genesis 32:24 Jacob wrestled with the angel until he was blessed. We need to wrestle with the angel and refuse to let him go until he blesses us! We need to pray all night and day and do whatever it takes to receive a blessing. More importantly we need to wait on the voice of the lord. That's the biggest part is waiting. Matthew 7:7 says "Ask, and it shall be given you; seek, and ye shall find; knock and it shall be opened unto you." but after you have done all you know to do just wait and let God move and watch him perform a miracle for you.

Addiction and Depression

All addictions are the same. The need or want to feel better than you do right now; a craving or yearning to feel good. But what void is there that you're trying to fill? What are you missing? I know that pain can cause you to do almost anything to get relief. When you stub your toe you jump around holding it screaming but does it really help? When you smash your finger you put it in your mouth does that help? You do all kinds of things to feel better: sit in the sun, go on vacation, shop or go to the beach, so what happens when you feel sorry for yourself? We talk about the outside of your body being cleaned up what about the inside? When you're sad what do you do?

When your depressed you think oh no one loves me, what about mad or hurting? Sometimes feelings and emotions can be more than our human body can handle.

When my first wife told me she had cheated on me my emotions were what have I done wrong? Then I became angry. How could she betray me this way? How does a person overcome such betrayal and heartache? You have to learn to redirect your emotions just like you had a bad day and you come home and take it out on your family. I'm not saying take it out on the person but rather do what makes you feel better. What has occurred is that your self-esteem is low, your confidence is low. You feel like you wasted your life. You have to get away, take a break, and reflect on your life, you may need a new perspective on things. Be sure to find yourself because things are about to change. If you can work it out great but if not move on but something is going to change.

No matter what happens you have to forgive, the

weight of sadness and depression is too heavy to carry by yourself. Have you ever noticed how easy it is to forgive when both of you are at fault and when you both come clean? But to do something after you know something about your spouse or significant other is wrong. Revenge is never the answer. I have looked through the bible to try and find an answer to emotional pain. Jesus healed our physical pain but what about deep pain, deep hurt, church hurt, and betrayal. Pain so deep it feels as if your heart is bleeding, when you find yourself in deep depression. I've been there more than I like to admit and I've asked God where I went wrong. What have I done? I have tried to serve God with all my heart, live as clean as I know how, pray, read my bible, and repent daily but now what?

I am still hurting. My second wife died from a blood clot in her brain, three days later my children were taken away to stay with their biological father and grandparents. Once again I asked where I went wrong. Not only was I dealing with my loss my life had started over again. Oh the pain! Where was my God? Where was Jesus? One year later do I date? Do I just focus on God? I was lost and I mean really lost. What do you do when everything in your life is not as it seems? I just celebrated Christmas no tree, no presents, no family or friends, and no visits. What is Christmas if there is no one to share it with? I wonder sometimes if this is what death feels like. What is life without hope? Why live without a dream? So I start dreaming of a house full of family and laughter and presents under an enormous tree and hoping one day this will be so. All we can do is hope things will get better because it can't get any worse once you hit rock bottom. Everything I once had is gone but I have accepted the Lord giveth and the Lord taketh away, but yet I live. I will see a brighter day because I still have breath and I know that God has not forgotten about me.

Fasting (Matthew 6:16)

Right now I am on a church fast, at the beginning of

the year our church as a whole goes on a fast for different needs but the one thing that I have learned is God does not take pleasure in our suffering. I heard some say "I'm going three days without eating or drinking." God is a loving God all he requires of us is to present our bodies a living sacrifice. When I'm on a fast I pray Lord how do I eat today? Like today he said take a potato boil it in with bell peppers and salt and pepper, cook with only water in this fast and no meat. Then I microwaved the potato when it was almost done boiling. I had the soft potato the skin was dry and I ate it with salt and honey crackers, and the peppers were great and I was full. I felt the presence of the lord so strong.

Why do we make things so difficult? For the longest time I was a miserable Christian. Then one day the Lord spoke and said you have no vision for the church so you have no vision for the future. We have to ask ourselves what is important, what matters. We prepare our life like we are going to stay here forever. I'm sorry but death is coming ready or not. So what does a dead man worry about? If you notice everything works out for the good of those who love the Lord. In James 1:17 it says "Every good gift and every perfect gift is from above, and cometh down from the father of lights, with whom is no variableness, neither shadow nor turning." God said don't worry what you put on the flowers are clothed how much more are you? They don't spin nor toil don't worry about what you will eat look at the birds, they eat over two times their body weight and if you notice they eat all day and God says are you much greater than many sparrows? (Matthew 6:25-34). Why are we so stressed with no direction? No happiness and so much hurt. I tell you why because we don't say thank you God we don't praise and say oh what a great day God has made and thank you Lord for our food. I thank God for my family. Your name alone deserves the honor and glory and the praise. God is love.

While we are on the topic of love it says in first Corinthians chapter 13 verses 4 through 8 " Love is patient, love is kind. It does not envy, it does not boast, it is not proud. It is not rude, it is not self-seeking, it is not easily angered, it keeps no record of wrongs. Love does not delight in evil but rejoices with the truth. It always protects, always trusts, always hopes, always perseveres. Love never fails."

Forgiveness and Fear

You ever notice when asking what did I do wrong we never expect that bad things happen to good people. So what then? We start the blame game. We imagine a different story to hide the fact that some way it's our own fault too. Covering it up does not make it go away it only hurts the people around you more. Blaming God doesn't help either. It's better to face it, take the blame, and move forward. Forgiveness has more power than you think. Imagine a husband and wife both of them loving and caring, an ideal marriage. They have a child and the mother and father are enjoying time together in the living room, their child in its room. The mother enters the room to check on the child only to find the child dead. The mother screams hysterical when the father enters the room he screams what happened and what did you do? The mother screams she didn't know what happened and she didn't do anything. The father may start blaming the mother saying she should have checked on the child sooner. You should have done this you should have done that. Both of them hurt, both of them scared. Imagine the emotions and tension, with those facts who is at fault? Who is to blame? What is the opposite of blame? Forgiveness. Oh how close the husband and wife could be if they stop blaming each other. With forgiveness they can embrace each other cry with each other. No one wins when you wait on the other to make something right. Forgive and move on. Life is too short to waste being angry and holding grudges.

Another emotion that holds back the strongest man is fear. Fear is crippling. It will make you emotional, and physically handicapped. I was in a mess when it came to fear. I had so many strongholds it could not be counted. Now I am considered a Paranoid Schizophrenic. With fear its cause and effect you always see the effect being so dramatically life changing or something that is going to be painful. But our imagination causes us to see the effect of our fear to be worse than it really is. We have imagined or hallucinated a situation to be worse than it is and blows it way out of proportion. Fear becomes our master. We get scared of what people will say, scared of pain, of germs, of getting hurt or rejects. The results are catastrophic. When we allow fear to rule us and yes it rules us, it becomes our enemy.

I love to sing. I go to every practice, I go to class but when it is time to stand in front of the church and sing I stay in my pew. I am a former drug addict and because I was a long term user the drugs ate away at my teeth. So I use the excuse if I open my mouth people will see my teeth. Then I say I am shy, everyone will be staring, and lastly they sound great already without me. I have an excuse for everything! By shutting out singing I shut myself out of opportunities. I made it where God could not use me so I have bondage there. There is a part in my life I cannot go to. There is a place in my life where I am not welcome. Can you believe that we can put ourselves into bondage and lose what could be the most joyful time of our lives and the truth is no one is even thinking about the excuses I have. They could care less about my teeth. What the enemy wants is to steal and kill my praise but if I would just step out of my comfort zone and begin to sing for God not caring what I look like or what the people may be thinking I would see God work in my life, and you would too. Whatever you do don't let the enemy steal your praise.

Jealousy

We often feel like we are being left out and when that happens we feel jealous. This is a self-esteem problem. It has nothing to do with the other person involved, it's like being picked last on the basketball team, you just don't feel good enough and you may be a really good player but because you were picked last it affects your whole game. When you think about being jealous it's an emotion of not feeling good enough, really feeling left out. This adds stress to our lives. The pressure builds up like a water hose and when the weakest part is under the most pressure it explodes. What comes out is something that cannot be controlled. This stress is the reason why we have headaches, sickness, high blood pressure, strokes, heart attacks, and numerous other problems with our bodies.

A problem that our youth is dealing with now is bullying. Teens are emotional unstable as it is and their hormones are out of control so adding the stress of bullying only makes it worse. I understand because I suffered my whole life with these issues and never understood until I asked where I went wrong. With every action or stress there is a reaction or emotion. We are like pots on a stove when we get to our boiling point. We have to have time to cool down, reflect on how and what you are feeling; if not you are going to boil over onto every other part of your life. Think about the recent school shootings. We want to blame guns, no security, arm the teacher, and make stricter gun laws. All these excuses do is cover up the problem. I have had the same emotions as other mental patients which says nobody knows how I feel; I'm going to make them feel the same pain I do. But we have to see the signs of boiling point. Find help and let people know they are not alone.

It is the emotions and stressors of life that cause us to give up the same way you punch a hole in the wall, throw a book, or slam a door understand that we are only feeling emotions. Once we know what's causing our stress we move on. I won't feel this way tomorrow, we must not react so quick to stress. First reflect on how you are feeling, and what you are feeling. Then accept it and redirect it! Remember your first reaction is the correct one but the wrong one and it bothers you more than it hurts anyone else. The fire burns hotter and bigger the more you place on it, and sometimes the flame is so hot no one can stand to be around it and it's only controlled by how much you allow to be placed on it. But with an explosion of fire or a wildfire you have placed your problems on other people causing them stress which causes others stress till there's nothing left to destroy but itself. What kind of fire will you be?

Back to bullying, it is one of the most unstable roller coaster rides there could be. Peer pressure is a main contributor to this, but it doesn't only happen in bullying it can happen on the job, and on a date. No one is immune to this and there are many forms. We think of it as picking or fighting but it's much deeper than that. Bullying is anything that causes

another person to have to defend themselves so by that they are pressured to make a choice. For example your boss on the job every day comes by and has something negative to say. Maybe he's having a bad day so he's throwing gas on your slow burning fire. Imagine friends pressuring you to do something they think is fun but is dangerous. What about on a date where the girl is pressured to engage in intercourse before she is ready causing her to defend herself or give in so she doesn't get talked about. A million and one scenarios with the same outcome but how do you defend yourself without causing harm to yourself or others? You simply tell someone.

Tell a parent, or a teacher tell someone because if not you could get to your boiling point quicker than you thought.

It's important to know what you're feeling and why because any emotion can be triggered to cause a stress or emotion. Not dealing with these emotions can cause anger. This is one sign to look for in children. For the longest time I stayed depressed because I didn't know what I was feeling until I started writing down my emotions and feelings. We can be stressors in each other's lives and not even know it. We could be the bully and not even realize we are the problem. For example, the boss's child loses on his XBOX game, he screams at his mom, the mom fusses at dad before he goes to work then he takes it out on the employees, one employee goes home and fusses with his wife about his day, the wife hollers at the children about their room not being clean, the child walks outside and kicks the dog, and the dog runs off and bites the neighbor! Unless you take control where will it end? How many of us are affected by others emotions? Will you think next time you are under pressure, be the end of the boiling point, redirect your emotions and imagine a different reaction.

You know I spent the majority of my life not expressing my own feelings but reacting to others. I could be feeling good until "she" showed up she always has drama and always has problems so we spend most of our time trying to reason with "her" so she don't do anything stupid. Do you know this person? Every one of us does.

I set out to write this book to help us recognize how much we are controlled by our emotions and how others determine how emotional we get. Like when we go and buy a pair of shoes, the whole day you look at everyone else's shoes and say they need new shoes, those are nice but mine are better, oh I should have bought those. Remember, you can change your outcome by simply recognizing your emotions. I hope that you recognize that you are not always the problem and find coping skills to not only help you control your emotions but also help others.

Empty Place

Growing up I never thought I was different; I ate and played like other children but I finally realized I wasn't the same when I started school. After a few years I was placed in the special education class and I wondered what's so special? Why can't I go to class with the other children? I was able to visit the children I was once in class with when I stopped by to empty their trash cans. I would ask myself what I have done wrong. I was treated different so why not act different as well. I started getting in trouble all of the time and I loved the attention and besides, I could get away with it because I was "special."

No one ever stopped to ask what was wrong with me; no one ever took the time to tell me what was wrong with me either. Passing me along in school, the teacher would say take this test! What's a test? What is a book? If my school could have seen one thing about me I believe it would have made me special. I never forget anything like what I see, or what I hear I have a photographic memory. I never did any homework as a child but everything written on the chalkboard I can remember to this very day. I had no book sense but my intellect was out of the roof. I was finally tired of the abuse so I quit school and started at a military academy for troubled kids.

Because I went to military school I was able to take college courses. Remember I could barely read but in a years' time I had my high school diploma and two trades and I wasn't even sixteen years old. I stopped making excuses when I was in military school I learned how to act in public, and how to be a man. I developed different skills that helped me communicate better with different people. Can you believe this? It's all about your will. It's all about what you are willing to change, and willing to deal with. But my struggles did not end there, as a matter of fact, they were just beginning. It wasn't until I was out on my own that I really found out what stress and other people can do.

Finding Answers

I have a cat and a dog. My cat gives me all the affection and love, and my dog is my playmate, he brings out the kid in me. I throw the ball to him, we run together. I love both of my animals but when they are together, we have problems. I'm not willing to give up either one of them to have peace, plus they are like family and family will always fight. The dog will chase the cat, and sometimes the other way around! But when I come on the scene it is a fight for my affection. Animals really show their emotions and have personality. If I rub the cat the dog barks, rub the dog and that cat scratches and bites, and if you show either one a little attention it's never enough. Are we not the same way? Starving for attention and longing to be loved?

Many of us sell ourselves short just to be shown affection. Does anyone really care for me? Does anyone even know that I exist? Dwelling on these thoughts are what places us in depression, causes suicide, and promiscuous sex. Everyone is just longing to be loved. Think about the mess and tragedies we've encountered; all of the trouble relationships and unloving companionships and we stay in these unfulfilling, abusive relationships because we believe this is the best we can do. We fear being alone. When we are surrounded by negativity daily we start to believe that what we have feared is alive and this monster has kept us captive. Unfortunately sometimes the only way a person seems to be free from their torment is death.

I speak today to give you hope, I feel your pain. I was once that person, doing everything I knew to be expected, but it never came until I found peace with myself, until I realized for me to be truly happy is not to be accepted by others but to know I am strong, I am beautiful, and I am perfect in the sight of a loving God. I come to understand I'm not perfect and comparing myself to others only makes me feel worse. But I promise to do the best I can with my life.

Emotions Speak

Believe it or not, your emotions have a voice. Just like carrying on a conversation with a family member or a friend. Who are you to tell me I'm not loved? To tell me I'm not good enough? Telling me I could never do better? I thought I was the only one who heard voices but truthfully we all get a little manic sometimes. "I ought to slap your face"; "I could hurt someone!" Yes, call me crazy but you hear them too. The voices tell you to do all sorts of things but that's not who you are, you are not crazy. That is our emotions talking to us; sometimes actions speak louder than words. Dealing with our emotions is what makes our character. How we react to certain circumstances is how we are defined and remembered.

People will talk about you whether it is good or bad "That persons hot tempered, they will go off on you in a minute." Or "She's so nice she wouldn't hurt a fly." That's why I speak often in this book about reflecting on what you are feeling and react differently because nothing is so bad you should destroy your own future or implode and self-destruct. I know a man who was changing the oil in his car to take a trip out of town. He was unable to loosen the drain plug to drain out his oil; the more he tried the more upset he became. He finally took a hammer and beat the drain plug off then busted the windows out and proceeded to beat the whole car. The more damage that was done the angrier he became until finally he totaled his whole car. Something that could be so simple to some may be a breaking point for others. I could think of a million ways to help him and you probably could too but by destroying his car he ruined his trip. By blowing things out of proportion we can destroy our future. Finally, we can hurt other people causing them to react violently. Remember this: My attitude determines my altitude. With a bad attitude you will go nowhere and you only make the people around you uncomfortable but a good attitude is contagious, it spreads and brightens everyone's day and also draws people to you.

Life Changing

Through my disability I turned it into my ability to read other people; not only by their actions but by their responses. I made it my life's work to study human behavior, to notice people's ticks and their triggers. It's amazing what we carry around in us that controls our behavior; monkey see monkey do. Some of us carry the same traits as their parents which create a never ending cycle; truly we never really evolve by acting like some of the Neanderthals before us. But what seems to work is having the awareness of a higher power and holding ourselves accountable of our actions. First we have to come to the knowledge of truth.

We must have a law without a law. Sometimes we can have no sense of right or wrong and we must see that we are judged by the law and know that for everything we do there is a consequence. Without knowing this we have nothing to judge ourselves by and nothing to fear. People have no fear of the law unless the consequences are greater and worthy to be feared.

People are becoming more and more wicked because they don't have a healthy dose of fear. Nobody is making examples out of people anymore. Death seems to just be a way out. I think if there were public executions or something that would put fear in people there wouldn't be so many crimes. People do crimes and never think they will get caught or don't fear the consequences. I know this matter is sensitive but through my experiences I don't see anything being resolved and people need a sense of security that the laws that are before us are not only for our safety but for our protections also.

Give me Safety

I imagine some of you have never seen a family member murdered or a loved one raped or a helpless child abused and it may not even be a concern of yours but the story would change dramatically if that were your father, mother, or siblings. If the crime takes place in your family your heart would rage with anger. For example, a flood is not a concern to birds in the sky. They will just fly up to the trees and rest in their nests but the damage is to all the other animals below. Their food sources are destroyed. When a crime is committed it affects everyone in some way or another. The effects may not be great as others but truly all lives are changed forever.

When major tragedies take place like a school shooting it was in a lot of ways like a flood that damages a lot of homes. Many ask what happened to drive this person or that person to do such things. The problem was a man who wants to place his pain on others. A person who reached his boiling point. We don't know their stories or what set them off, or how they were affected as children but we know they have a lot of emotions and they may not have ever known how their lives and actions would affect so many. My love and support goes out to these families. We cannot change the past, but if we take action now, we can change the future

Reaching For the Stars

Reaching for the stars so high in the sky

If only that could be me who shines so bright

and be beautiful to everyone who sees

Only if I was a star, only if that was me.

Lovers would lay under me staring at my bright glare.

Little kids would make wishes and dream.

Everyone will wonder just what makes me shine so bright.

Astronauts would study me and come up for a closer look.

Only if that were me.

I would bring joy to everyone who sees, way

up there with no worries, no cares.

Only in the stars, if that could only be me.

But wait, who would miss one little star?

Out of billions, I ask who would wonder where I went?

Oh but life is still the same.

Admire me for a while but when the stars are gone

Who will miss them?

Dreaming of you (In memory of the Sandy Hook Children)

Oh my children, I know you went away.

I try to imagine that you are just outside to play.

You are a perfect vision of love, innocence,

pure forgiveness, and fun.

But my pain comes from the dreams I had for you.

It is like the sand at the beach, the

amount of hopes I prayed for you

For it is impossible to count them all.

I will remember you and watch you grow in my dreams.

I will holler out "Well done" when I see that you succeed

And cheer for you as you hit a homerun, and

clap for you when you dance at the prom.

In my heart you will live on; your mark

is forever infused in stone.

So now, live on.

Dedication

I would like to dedicate this book to Pastor Randy Simmons; my pastor, my mentor and my dearest friend. Also, to Holly Grove Holiness Church who taught me that no matter how hard the road and the struggles of life may be, keep on believing

Printed in the United States
By Bookmasters